SIMPLE BALANCE

(A Revelation, 40 Poems, and a Solitude)

SIMPLE BALANCE

(A Revelation, 40 Poems, and a Solitude)

Abdul Hadi Sadoun

Translated from Spanish by Lawrence Schimel

literalpublishing

First published in Spain in 2022 by Bala Perdida Editorial as *Sencillo equilibrio*. Published by agreement with Bala Perdida Editorial, S.L.

© 2024, Literal Publishing
5425 Renwick Dr.
Houston, TX, 77081
www.literalmagazine.com

This publication was supported in part by a grant from Acción Cultural Española (AC/E), a state agency.

AC/E
ACCIÓN CULTURAL
ESPAÑOLA

ISBN: 978-1-942307-61-7

Printed in the United States / Impreso en Estados Unidos

INDEX

For Kareem Sadoon
Brother and artist

"If to live is good
even better is to dream
and best of all, to wake."
—**Antonio Machado**

FIRST // A REVELATION

There is a time with the patina of age, which grants me the ability to think of your death in a surprising way. I think perforce of the al-Buraq, a mythological being, in the moment of the uncommon birth between the slowness of feet upon the ground or the flight of its misplaced wings.

There is a time to think of the emptiness that slows the path, in order to grant meaning to words and to the voices of a murmur that awaits them. Let us give to the facts our interest and our quarrels, while they are overcome with the agility of a bird.

There is a time for time itself, that which is at your side, in your trench, fortified by your companions, those who extend the oil in your lamp, only so that your eyes might light up for them. Meanwhile they surpass hundreds of miles, elongated, rounded, covered, and you keep them away without pain, nor rotation nor waiting. The affliction fills us without our fortifying ourselves with your oil.

There is ash, you scatter it with your turns. There is a common inheritance that we carry toward you and which transports our eyes in the foreheads of faces, searching for some rivers and the blackness of the south toward its north in order for us to toss within them your sheets and smell with it your mercy.

There is a fire that ignites in the sides, which now and in every beginning, asks me about you. I remember it in the pictures, in the pottery, and in the memory. He admires and examines. I tell him that the beginnings have made the flame eternal and they have blown out for themselves the fire. In the fire there is memory, one sees the truth without hindrance and there is no space for a later behind later.

SECOND // 40 POEMS

(1)

The Self

is the game

of the one who always

misses.

(2)

Immense labyrinths.
Years that don't return.

Your only footprint
competes
with the game
of the leaves that have fallen
due to such weight.

(3)

Our times intermingle

while I still remain

in that

posture.

I knead the colors

it might be that you approach

from your liquid

shape.

(4)

It is not like the desire to climb
nor the enthusiasm for getting lost.
The wheels
spin
and the head
like a net pointing upward
gathers
with a singular loyalty
the butterflies of the end.

(5)

The head is a head
and the letters are overflowing
with enigmas.

The growl
in
the shape
of a relaxed
dog
near the lance;
The circles lie ahead
and also behind.

(6)

Shaped
from the pain of the fingers
and the freedom of the clay,
hushed
in the reclining posture of my chair.

The yearning for reunion
moves
behind
yesterday's woods dyed
red.

(7)

A black spot.

I

and my desires hidden within it.

You

clarity stained

with my fingers

spread

behind

the lines

that break.

(8)

Cages of a burning
and glances
of the embers
of abstinence;
the feet elongate.

The bird
with the sign
of failure,
its time
is the curve
of a mute
letter.

(9)

More than thirty
and less than three,
the number
does no justice
to the desire of a long
howl
from a mouth
jagged
by torment.

(10)

From behind
there is nothing more
that a dotted back.
In the front
more than a dot
that wants to take shape.
A fascinating picture
contains one hundred nightingales
and twenty plums
with their branches
intertwined.

The rear and the anverse.

(11)

The head again

and a face that doesn't resemble my face.

Darkness,

responsible

for staining

the features

of a wall

searching for

its desired

color.

(12)

The games are over
save for yours
that has no end.
Concern for the inverted
complete vision.

(13)

Yearning for the shine of the eyes

the glimmer of the eyes

the half-closing of the eyes;

the flower is incomplete

without your scent,

and the window

far away

and full of

chimeras.

(14)

A head dialogues with the beam
from the lighthouse
the truth of the weak
and my chair
are nights
of a shattered
soul.

The lighthouse
is a sound
and the words,
a bouquet
snatched
from its desire.

(15)

Acrobats.

One acrobat.

Space

is a foretold

reminder

of the acrobatics

of life.

(16)

The difficult tests
bark in their interior. Fallacious shapes
and bodies the color of ether;
Always,
what we defend
underneath
our throbbing
fear.

(17)

My confidant is the meeting
my confidant
with the number of dots drawn
and the number of wild formations.

My confidant
with neither whisper
nor description.

Whiteness
that is remembered
with merciless
chills.

(18)

There are no wheels that roll
toward Man;
the course
to the shore.
Whoever made the others,
what is the fate of the world,
lacking tenderness
and static.

(19)

The kiss,
fireworks
that don't explode.
The faces,
another climb
toward the beginning.

Hey, goddess!
Erase us from your blessings
and from the transit
of your solemn wheel.

(20)

What does **trench** mean?
You contemplate it cautiously
when there is no one
around;
after, you massage
the exhaustion
of the chair
and its lazy
years.

(21)

He who is above
without a specific name;
He who is below
with no visible name.

Grids of light
nothing more.
A stomach
to reveal
desire
dilated
to the threshold.

(22)

In the company of gamblers

we need a staircase of astonishment

and we also need

two long legs

like a sea bird;

and the shine of an eye

like the dove's blue

as well

to search for

the meaning of the landscape

which we keep watch over

in the distances.

(23)

Plenty of heads

each a leap from a hole

and your head is the only one

smiling

settles on its usual seat:

White

is the empty

seat

like absence itself.

(24)

Only for today
do we remove our repeated faces
and out on
the masks
of a wandering
salvation.

(25)

Fingers interwoven
like a long-lived tree
without a murmur
nor a word
of reproach:
the living room jug
souvenir of a long ago encounter.

(26)

Is there someone who listens
in the mix of the dots
and the restlessness of the seductive answers?

The wheels turn
more than my elation
or my joy.

(27)

The surfaces come together.

Nothing is blacker than in the night

when my heart

is an eraser,

devours your mouth

pressed shut with uncertainties.

(28)

Our meeting seems a haiku:

the kiss, embroidered from a carpet,

the two mouths, with their eternal silence.

(29)

I am not predisposed

to shape my worlds.

No other shape

exists now for my world

save

for these

scattered

circles

that surround me.

(30)
A balcony,
hole.
To peer out
or a rigid
refuge
movable
with patience.
An artist
usually
classifies
tasks.
The desire
to disappear
deliberately
behind
the lines
with neither end
nor beginning.

(31)

We turn everything
into a simple balance
while we keep wandering
the labyrinth that names the things
that don't know one another.

Our alliance
is the twists link.

(32)

I return once more
pushing my dreams
backwards
searching for protection
on the wheel of life.

Bent over
I glimpse you.
You are the path,
the path,
the path.

(33)

From what point does movement begin?

The sun is there
inert stone
without avail.

(34)

I see you there

in my other eye,

and because you don't see me

while

I want

toward my barracks,

which are armed to the teeth

with reproaches.

(35)

I lean toward you,

you lean toward me,

the next pool

has no water

and the wandering cloud

has no shape that embraces it.

I lean…

You lean…

(36)

The size of the line
my horizon
is the same
as the door
of hope
riddled by
bulletholes.

The howl
is the poor man's jug
in the night of the end.

(37)

My acrobatics superimpose themselves

erotic

vertical

and my horizon

like a non-stop flight,

a relentless

rest.

The two heads

are two bridges

with no passageway.

(38)

Bangle
without jingling
like how a whale
leaps
over the barbed wire,
your soft
pillow.

I cross toward you
through the holes
of the anaesthesized city.

(39)

Only one body

and two horrifying movements

two desires

interwoven without welding

I was one of them

and the other was not you.

The window is now closed,

it reveals its bitter

assurance

without calculation.

(40)

The eye, again
and at last:
an orifice of light
a watching circle
of points of harmony
and separation.

The eye observes
an evident presence;
the presence:
Both,
with no one else,

FINAL // A SOLITUDE

Like an explicit idea that encourages you to be reconciled
with what is to come; a shout that no one hears; an
emptiness that surrounds you and that perhaps you
surround;

those who search for light in the darkness; a straight line in
drawing objects distorted by an unnecessary twist;

no longer a dilemma of their world; it will be in a name that
is not isolation; an empty word like a hollow drum; sterile
shouts that don't even reach further than the throat.

To live like a prehistoric object; its clay tablet recounts the
stones of its cave; paint free, the giraffe of the stretched
dreams.